On the Midnight Shores

Victor Hu

BookLeaf Publishing

India | USA | UK

Presentation by *BookLeaf Publishing*

Web: www.bookleafpub.com

E-mail: info@bookleafpub.com

ISBN: 978-93-5744-760-7

First edition 2022

DEDICATION

Dedicated to Sara, without whom these poems would not have born fruit.

PREFACE

To write poetry is to pick flowers by the roadside - to gather a posy of other men's flowers along a journey of one's own.

These poems comprise the collected and curated works of five years. Although I never intend so, I find it almost impossible to avoid writing autobiographically - perhaps this is why I always feel my writing to be too telling.

Consequently, this may be the most accurate possible expression of myself, something I could never have shared had it not been for the encouragement of my loving partner and the relative comfort of anonymity.

Thank you for taking the time out of your day to peruse these arrangements of words I have to offer - I sincerely hope they should bring you some enjoyment, if not prove valuable in their own right.

The Fish-Men

And so the great and vaulted sky was cleaved in
two.
Its puffy clouds, like startled sheep, did flee the
source
From whence the heavens yawned – as crack of
dawn had too
Once yawned like opened door. Yet now the
weathered wood
Had splintered and been shattered forth by
unknown force.
And through the darkling chasm, like the night,
there would
Outpour the monsters of the deep, whose scaly
hides
And bulging eyes – like bloated moon snatched
from her seat –
Glowed with uncanny hue. The shades of green
that tides
Adorn, forlorn unseen demanding that man's
sight
Be cast upon their form, now did spill forth to
sleek
And shining fall. With quick and precipitous
flight

The creatures darted through the laden air made
thick
With fear that rose in pungent waves from far
below,
Where desperate men emerged. Against their
fate they kicked
And screamed – the bubbles of their cries rose
high unto
The deafened riders wreathed with otherworldly
glow –
Who, in appearance almost saintly, downwards
flew.
Against the spreading terror, twisting weed of
hell
That seized the heavens, men of science who
proclaimed
Their mastery over nature cowered. As had fell
That son of hubris, now the father awed as well
With reason tamed, before this ancient evil lame,
And final thought engulfed by frantic tolling
knell.

Fire

The flick'ring of our idle flame must end.
For all about do twilit shapes now creep
E'er closer to the ailing light, my friend.
And soon the chill will reach with ashen touch
To freeze the tears upon your cheek, so weep
No more, your grief is spent in vain. Too much
Has prov'd the price of our despondency;
This malcontent – the progeny of strife
And pettiness. It is a mutiny
Of spirit that tears now at our breast, therein
Which lies a radiant, fiery love of life
That yet does blaze unabashed. Recall within
That fierce, unyielding passion – ours by right!
That echoed forth when we were born so full
Of hope and faith in dawn that follows night!
Recall that light which has grown dim with time,
But once did blaze within your eyes so full
Of fight! One thousand sorrows could not find
A single scrap of doubt within you then, –
Then when the sun rose high upon your chin
And all revolved around you, dearest friend.
So nevermind this darkness, it will pass,
You are my brother, dearest of all men,
The flick'ring of our idle flame must end.

Ode: To Destiny

And who are you, old friend, to know me so?
To brush aside that lie, my weak disguise,
And lift the darkened soot that clouds my soul?
Born witness to each joy and leaden sigh
Which wracked this mortal shell, why do you
call?
Your ever-present cue which ever-true
Does point towards some fixéd mark beyond
My weakened sight. Let fall
The curtains on this act, now bid adieu -
What reason is there now to struggle on?

Each fleeting day grows weak upon the vine
Which once did bear such able-bodied fruit -
Once vibrant, full of earthly joy, now pines
Away. Corruption courts those twinéd roots -
Once incorrigible, now shy, unsure.
Long have I ceased to mark the tolling hour;
The rising sun finds not my patronage
Nor darkness my censure.
I have, within this lucid dream, no power –
The past lies still, entombed upon the page.

O for the courage now to battle on!
With stoic mind and heart hence anchored in

One firm belief, one point which thus upon
This tired soul can hang. Oh grief, you pin
My sins upon my breast akin to knives
Within my heart. Yet others cannot see
The foul ignominy that lies within,
From whence there does derive
The death of all that charms. Where hope does
flee
And sorrow takes its curséd home therein.

What sorry eulogies I weave; to play
The Siren to my own demise. Each word,
An empty pledge for easeful death to lay
My sorrows and my worries by his side.
This light against the darkling sky grows dim,
The ancient night does cast her veil to guide
Me t'ward that warm embrace. Too long, I fear,
Have I so tempted him –
Yet wrists unsplit, my sweetened words did lie –
That guilty blush still secretly held dear.

In even this I prove myself a fiend!
To cling to that which I bemoan as might
An infant to a teat! What life is glean'd
When e'en the self is loathed? If merely spite
I would have flaggéd long ago, no pride
Of such does set my spirits thus aglow.
Nor love of life, who thus hath taught me naught
But pain, and did misguide

At every chance to birth my present woe.
Those prophet's words that hidden perils
wrought.

What else sustains this languid march but you?
You who hath stayed the scythéd hand of debt;
Assayed and found this bastard to be true –
Though many troubles have my path beset.
Whence did I earn this faith that you bestow?
Your voice from precipice and peak alike,
Hath pulled me back with firm but gentle lilt,
And soothed my passions low,
To gesture t'ward some further, unseen height.
With promise of a future to be built.

I cannot see that place where you have been –
Yet in my mind, where fancy nurtures hope,
And hope gives shape to half-forgotten dreams,
A glorious world therein is set aglow.
Beyond the darkling chasm of the night,
Beyond the ceaseless warring thoughts that
press,
Beyond this present prison of the mind
I trust that you are right.
With courage now to struggle on, to test
This providence so born of your design.

Sonnet: To Eternity

Thy beauty is through absence best described;
The gentle blooms of June asleep in May,
The absence of the gilded light of day.
It is this nameless absence night decries,
When streams of moonlit tears adorn the skies,
When flame of heaven hides his crown away,
And flowers don their mourning colours grey.
Then to all things a restless rest's proscribed.

So sleepeth not immortal jewel of life!
Now dance thy beauteous dance until the end
Of time! Now in Elysium's vibrant fields,
Where new eternal blooms know not of strife;
Where dawn to dusk its brilliant vigour lends,
And fire need not to the ashes yield.

The New Olympians

The hazy mist of Morpheus did flush
My feeble sense. And through these sleep sealed eyes
I saw an awing sight that drew a blush
Upon the distant, deep, and darkling skies.
The castles of The New Olympians
There grew, resplendent and magnificent
Fantastic – grand divine! What words can call
Into the mind that realm of champions!
And through the oculus of lucent sleep
I watched and nearly wept upon it all.

Great pillars bearing down upon the earth
As if from heaven plunged into the ground.
And on the mighty stones of unknown worth
Rose murals of the turbulent profound.
The finest measures of some ancient tale,
Whose glory would the boldest feats of Greece
And Rome fast call to shame, here did resound.
Its infinitely complex lines must hail
Of some unmatched, unfathomed expertise,

With knowledge of some truth e'en more
profound.

And vaulted ceilings loomed above the stars,
Suggesting at the Titans dwelling here
Whose vast and ancient legs of thickened bark
Must seize firm root upon the floor; whose sheer
And noble brows must share the company
Of heaven. Curtains fell like waterfalls
O'er miles of tumbling silk – though I know not
If it were silk or some more godly cloth.
And hues unknown to man stretched through the
halls,
Which reason, at the slightest glimpse, besot.

Perhaps this world of forms has blessed few men
Before. In fables of Tír Tairngire
And other whispered, mystic lands of lore,
Where shadows of a recognition lay.
O shadow! Such now cuts across my mind
And chills me to the core! From reverie
I wake the eyes that envy rendered poor.
And, banishing my admiration blind,
Now gaze upon the terror plain to see –
A thought that brings a shudder to the fore:

For might these mighty New Olympians,
Share in the wretched, squalid thoughts of men?

Sonnet to Music

I never should have brought my music here -
To this unnatural place, where truth is shunned
And talent shamed. That purest song held dear
To heart through pettiness and spite profaned.
For music true needs not its merit prove –
And, like a lover's kiss, needs no excuse.
Its origin lies in a soul once moved
To lay its bleeding passions for the muse.
The music here is not music at all –
Is broken, bent, and suffering for truth.
It answers, placid, to a master's call –
Is young, though lacking in the soul of youth.
I never should have brought my music here,
This frigid bastion of the insincere.

Study on E. Poe's "The Raven"

'Twas a day like any other, as I searched the
junk and clutter,
That bedewed my attic room like silver drops
upon the morn.
There the dust that danced and glistened in the
early light did listen
Seemingly to music hidden as they twirled about
the floor.
Dust that danced in graceful lines that I had
never seen before,
Hinting, then, at something more.

Though the day was young and sprightly, and all
round was painted lively
Life and light, the darkened nightly shadows
banished from the floor,
I did not feel quite so easy, to be true e'en
slightly queasy
For the darkened shadows lingered still upon my
spirit's core,
For the fretful memories of terror that had come
before

Lingered still, there evermore.

For the spectre visited me; though only a
moment stayed he,
In that momentary glimpse I saw a truth that I
abhorred:
That the son should follow father, heedless of
want or disaster
Follow farther, follow faster was to be my only
store.
Such a fate is worse than death as many men
have known before,
Wand'ring through an opened door.

Out of fright I fled my sorrow, seeking here
perhaps to borrow
From these antiquated hollows of the happy days
of yore
Some resemblance of order, here amidst the rank
disorder,
Yet these trinkets of the past could not induce
my soul to soar.
And the moment I stepped through the darkened
frame of attic door,
Heavy sigh I did outpour.

Here I felt my shoulders shaking and to still that
fearful quaking,

As if from some trance awaking sought some
purchase on the floor.
"Surely" cried I "Surely there is some solution
for this sickness
That afflicts me – that now grips me like the
Erinyes of lore.
Some Nepenthe that will save me from that grim
and ghastly door –
Open now forevermore."

Suddenly I heard a thumping, though not of the
sanguine pumping,
Starting me almost to jumping were I not upon
the floor.
Open hence before me yawning like the fiery
heavens dawning
Sudden revelation awning from a book upon the
floor –
From an ancient, antiquated album of the days of
yore,
Resting there and - nothing more.

Gathering my wits about me, reaching over e'er
so lightly,
Did I rest the album softly with the dawn's light
spilling o'er.
And perusing with great caution this unbidden
apparition

That did seem with divine mission to have
chanced upon the floor
Liberation or perdition resting on my attic floor,
Tortured me like ne'er before.

Presently my soul succumbing to the doubts that
were becoming
What if I should glance and but confirm the writ
I drew before?
Fearing thus my mind did wonder to that place
were terrors ponder
Somewhere past the threshold yonder where
sanity holds its store –
Where against the tides of terror reason holds its
fragile store
Meeting hell's infernal roar.

And the world was painted evil as if by some
unseen devil
That had risen, foul born from the fears that
rotted at my core.
And the sky no longer sprightly, and the light no
longer lively
Seemed now to me so unsightly, gaunt and
ghastly from the floor –
From my perch, my home of sorrow, lying
helpless on the floor
Next to that prime-evil lore.

I could not recall my courage, it had fled the
coloured visage
Pallor printed, past my placid perjured form
upon the floor.
Eagerly I wished time's arrow would permit me
now to borrow
Some brief respite from my sorrow, sorrow for
the task before –
For the Sisyphean feat that rested at the
mountain's fore,
Doomed for now and evermore.

But my cowardice prevailing, for the fear of
never knowing
Seemed a terror e'en more frightening than that
which I brooded o'er.
Lifting forth my tired gaze I saw as if through
thickened haze my
Manner there upon the page imposed upon the
father's form.
Likeness mine as clear as ice, a truth that chilled
me to the core,
Doomed for now and evermore.

All the features that presented were those which
I had resented,
Thickened brow, the visage, and the trace of hair
that laid before.

All the features now assented what my soul had
so dissented,
That the fates had now consented to consign me
to the core –
Given up and so abandoned to that curséd,
opened door
Doomed for now and evermore.

And my spirit was forsaken, all the fight within
me taken
but for something that did draw my focus on the
page before.
Yes, the thickened brow, the visage was the
same I had envisaged
But the eyes! The blessed eyes were not the
same I thought I saw!
Yes, those eyes, their different tint, a glint that
saved me from the door!
Saved me now and evermore!

And the light by God grew lighter, and the
horrors were no longer,
All within me, from within me had the terrors
come before!
Leaping from my lowly burrow purpose clear
and here unfurrowed
Newly born this life, tomorrow's triumph was to
be my store!

Never would I lose this sight returned from
yonder opened door
Triumph now and evermore!

Sonnet: To Death

We are, in truth, the creatures born of death.
Our father is the skipping of the hour;
Our mother is the dark from which we cower.
The light of life is not our rightful hearth
Such is the fated nature of our birth.
This truth oft whispered by the fading fire,
As darkling shadows creep towards the pyre,
And slowly slows the beating of our breath.

Yet we should not fear passage to that place,
Feel terror hounding at our snuffing pulse,
Nor apprehension at the dying light.
For deepest sleep does bring us face to face –
With truth; dispels this quaint illusion false;
Returning us, at last, to veiled night.

Elegy: To Friendship

Look at us now, my friends!
Who once could laugh so free
in youth, in spite of time,
in spite of all – at ease.
O how good things may end,
my friends, O how good times
must cease. That which was born
from clay will die as dust;
each fleeting joy is met
by pain – O such it must!
Yet still my heart is torn;
the wound there will not set.

Do you recall to mind
those memories as I?
Drawn from the archives with
a smile – O how they lie!
So sweetly do they bind
my fancy – though as myth
Of foreign times, seem far
Too gilded to be truth.
Yet t'is a lie I would

Embrace – forget the truth!
His price I cannot bear,
Nor would I if I could.

Those days when sorrow played
the understudy to
good cheer; when kindred smiles
were never far from view
and kindred voices made
good company a while.
Those days are gone, my friends,
what now remains? What might
we do save keep a strong
and stoic face; to play
the part that time has lent
and grieve away from sight?

A tear for every friend I've lost to fate,
to time, to realisation come too late.
Though all the tears within me would not do
As memory to even one of you.

Study on Homer's Iliad Book 21

Woe that now streaks to the once bright Ilium
gates of old Altes;
Phoebus Apollo the archer, distant and deadly,
has tired
Of Priam's children, their rich cuts of oxen that
peel from the white bone;
But, now, favouring that of the bronze-haired
Achaens, he turns deaf
Hearing not cries from the widows of Troy he
now faces away. Fast
Seeks now son of King Peleus quick to his mark
as a vulture,
Arrow that flies to the crumbling walls sure to
buckle and falter.

Lone leans the shield of the Trojans yet
gleaming well-oiled in bronze, that
Helmet now catching the fiery glow of the
murderous sun. He
Sees that the Hounds of Orion, foaming now
bounding now clustered,

Closing in tight for the kill flashing fangs buried
deep into Taurus.
And the aging old bull tiring of his pursuit here
turns head high,
Seeking the palace of wide-seeing Zeus – who
marshals the thunder –
Wild-eyes wide and the sweat matted brow now
calling in pain 'O
Why have you turned from me father of all – I
who once held your favour –
Muscles now aching now failing I hear wingéd
death sweeping near, here
Seeking to bear me away from the skies that I
knew as my home! Now,
Lost and abandoned by all like a shield which is
weathered and cracked wide,
Splintered and worn of no use anymore to be
thrown to the far side!"

Farther above in the high-backed tower atop
those great walls sat
Kingly old Priam his frail figure burdened by
royal adornment,
Sapphires sapping those irises pale and rubies
that stole the
Lustre from cheek, yet gripped firm the
well-gilded rests of the hard seat.
Waiting behind him with face wet and breast
bare was Hecuba, grieving,

Already mourning the death of her son, that dearest by far of
All Priam's princes, that child she reared on her own loving milk, that
Boy she had nursed with her own soft hands whom the coarseness of service
Never had touched. Further still, seeking shadows to hide her from sight, to
Cover that radiant beauty unfit for the suffering soul, hid
Helen of Sparta, for cursed is the woman who flees from her duty,
Gives up her father and husband, abandons most sacred of oaths to
Seek out for comfort a soft, foreign bed. And, many a time had
Women of Troy looked upon her in shame, turning quickly away as
Helen, that prize from a far distant land, wandered lone through the broad streets,
Calling to Hermes from ages away. They pitied her, poor wretch,
Broken by gifts from the gods and the passions of men which they knew too.
Yet still they hated her, she who had brought all the long racing ships with
Bristling ranks of strong-greaved Achaens all ready to wage war,

She that had snatched the children away from
their homes, from their bedsides.
No small thing a child to those noble women of
Troy. No
Princes had they nor princesses to teach not to
muddy their skirts, to
Braid well their hair, but one child is all, and for
what? Just to nurse, care,
Love so that black death looming may sweep
them away and in joy share?

How could they guess at the anguish, the turmoil
that wore at those crowned thoughts?
Fears which had led that daughter of Zeus to cry
out in blindness,
Quick when escaping from Oneiroi's box, that
assertion of life, breath
Given its dance through the cold, deathly air,
though no comfort would come "O
Woe that which streaked from those far-flung
lands! Those ships armed with strong men
Bearing me far from the soft earth of
Lacedaemon my first home!
Woe that the fiery trees ever fell and so
furnished to hand those
Oars that brought me here, to the Scaean Gates!
What a fool I
Am to have chosen this fate! Let none now
assert that the deathless

Gods show no mercy to us – they furnish our
hearts with desires,
Passions that burn quick to flame yet leave to us
still a sound mind. And
Even the fates may weave for us all two threads:
one to choose though
Both lead to suffering! O had I not then desired
and reached for
Paris's hand from that goddess of lust when she
stood at my door. Yet,
Is it so wrong, so hateful to seek out that wish to
be free? Yes,
I have taken for master that curse of all men and
this horrid
War as my child now I know it well that this
burden is my own.
Guilt I shall wear as my crown when my soul
seeks the black House of Death. Yet,
Guilt not for choosing my fate but for daring to
cross that hubristic
Ego of man that would set to his daughter the
cruel edge of black death,
Arrogant ego of man that would send deep-sea
ships off to kingdoms
Far – half the world away! War is my
punishment cruel that I dared to
Question the strong will of man, e'en the
deathless gods gave me choice; what

Choice did I have at the hands of bold Theseus
half-born divine who
Seeking a trophy desired my youth? When the
powerful sons of
Atreus came what could I have done but submit
as their prize? Plucked
Fast from my home as a fish from the stream to
be taken away. This
Beauty this gift from the gods is a curse for no
further do men look
If they should find, at a glance their desire, a
prize for the strong hook.

Terrible thoughts that must plague the daughter
of Zeus who now looks on
Seeing that herald of death seeking fast as an
arrow to pull down
Ilium's walls. Now the lone shield of Troy
stands in vain by the gates, men
Gleaming in bronze with swords flashing, spears
heralding shadowy death, fresh
Blood seeping down to the caverns below as the
sharpened blades pierce flesh.

The Weaver

She draws the heart-strings of her thread,
weaves nerve, sinew,
and flesh.
Each strand a eulogy delivered
by blood-stained hands.

Niobe

Time ages and grows old,
      mortal burdens are laid to rest,
      boulders cease their toil,
      and vultures tire of their prey.
The starved are satiated,
      and the satiated starved.
Boundless rivers wane
      and eternal fields empty.
Gods forget and rest,
      and yet a mother's sorrow is
remembered,
      wishing, in vain, that unyielding stone
      may finally open to her bitter tears.

Beneath the Elm

Even the children of day may forget themselves.
Bright hues of blue and green -
    a lover's eyes,
    a serpent's coat -
    hidden away wear grey.
So one dream-world fades,
    so another world is born.
The eyes adapt;
    even blackness has its shades.

The Great Race

The wild clamour of the starting line,
Blow of the starting gun ringing
In the brilliant morning sun – blazing,
Sweat-drenched brow, legs leading leaden,
Flagging, aching in this epic race.
Fists pumping, punching through the laden air,
Shoulders ramming, arms jostling,
Vision narrowed on the great blue,
That destination somewhere down the line.

Such were the frantic, precocious, eager opening
bars,
Yet, now, so many years upon this track,
The runners have all filtered out like
Ants across the distant, sun-bronzed
Horizon…
Now, so many years upon this track,
The swirling dust and cool kisses of the wind
Blowing across these still, timeless plains –
Now, so many years upon this track,
The bloodied, beating heart slowing,
Muscles mending, mind clearing, eyes seeing
For the first time,
The calm joys of living.
Now…

After all these years and all this distance run
Without seeking for a cause or asking how,
What, when, where, or why –
Life can finally begin.

Silent Words

I sat down one day,
At a desk subsumed by shadows,
And found I couldn't write.

Silent words upon an absent page,
Staring into an emptiness so complete,
Tumbling into an untitled grave.

And on the midnight shores
Of the recesses of my mind,
I search for him:
in the sand,
Beneath the waves,
Between the twinkling stars,
Of an obsidian sky.

Summer

It's a bright Summer's day today,
Or,
At least it feels like Summer.

I feel worn,
Like,
A pair of well-worn boots,
Or,
Sanding paper that has gone all smooth,
From being rubbed too much.

I feel tired,
Like,
I've woken up at the bottom of the sea,
And,
Gone right back to sleep,
In the soft sand.

Here there are no darling buds of May,
And the few that brave the cold
Have since faded.
Away,
And back again the sleepy
Dull-eyed trance of being,
Echoes.

Here, in the dark
Against the waves.

But it feels like Summer may at last arrive,
Into the warmth…
This time – I think she'll stay.

Floating

Floating beneath the twisting waves
Of this rich cerulian hue.
Eyes wandering, tracing satin curls,
To the subtle curves of her hips,
And that place where the delicate fabric
Folds.

Time

The rain taps against the glass,
The entrance to our storm-drenched
Sanctuary,
Music plays, voices softly speak,
Two hearts beat
At the confluence of timeless eternities.
Outside, the universe quietly waits
On the tender heartstrings of our love.

Optimism

I stood against the darkness of the night and
watched my breath
Unfurl. It seemed to me the essence of my being,
my spirit,
Unshaped, untamed, unsure, but free. A small
and momentary peace,
Graceful in its honesty, offering its gentle
warmth
To an endless, loving emptiness. And as I
watched
It filled me with a childish joy, a quiet
happiness,
As if the night had whispered secrets just for me.
And as
It slowly faded from the world, its lingering
warmth remained
The essence of my being, against the gentle
darkness of the night.